Easy K Cookbook

Innovative & Easy Ketchup Recipes You

Can Create at Home

BY

Carla Hale

License Notes

Table of Contents

Introduction

This book, Ketchup Cookbook is geared to change your life forever, if you really love ketchup! If you are up to the task of cooking an onion until it is sweet, then adding tomatoes and your own touch with your preference of herbs and spices; simmering and stirring until thick, rich and shiny, then you are on your way with your own creative version of making ketchup. It is so simple, quick and easy, from start to finish it is just about 30 minutes and a shelf life of about 30 days – though I am sure it will be finished before then.

Grabbing a bottle from the store might be easier but the taste of your own version is guaranteed!

Come on, get started and discover how your life can be changed in a positive way.

Horseradish Ketchup

An easy recipe to perk up your food.

Yields: 1 cup

Time: 5 minutes

Ingredients:

- Worcestershire sauce (1 tsp.)
- Garlic powder (1/4 tsp.
- Onion powder (1/4 tsp.)
- Vinegar (1 ¾ tbsp.)
- Water (3 tbsp.)
- Horseradish (2 ½ tsp)
- Juice (2 tsp.)
- Salt (1/3 tsp.)
- Pepper (1/4 tsp.)
- Brown sugar (2 ½ tbsp.)
- Tomato paste (6 oz.)

Directions:

1. In a medium bowl, mix all the ingredients together. Stir thoroughly until mixture is smooth.

2. Once you have received desired consistency, pour in a sterilized jar and refrigerate.

Cumin Seed Ketchup

This ketchup is very tasty and is perfect for hamburgers, grilled steak and just about anything that is grilled.

Yields: 1 2/3 cups

Time: 1 hour 45 minutes

Ingredients:

- Salt (1/2 tsp.)
- Cayenne pepper (1/4 tsp.)
- Dry mustard (1/2 tsp.)
- Peppercorns (6, black)
- Celery seeds (1/2 tsp.)
- Whole cloves (1 tsp.)
- Cumin seeds (1 tsp.)
- Yellow mustard seeds (2 tsp.)
- Cinnamon (1 stick)
- Sugar (1/4 cup)
- Cider vinegar (1/2 cup)
- Garlic (2 cloves)
- Yellow onion (1/2 medium)
- Plum tomatoes (2 cans, whole peeled)

Directions:

1. Put the tomatoes, onion and garlic in a blender. Blend until smooth. Strain the mixture and dispose of solids.

2. Meanwhile, let tomato mixture simmer in a large pot over medium low heat. Cook until mixture has been reduced to half, roughly about 1 hour.

3. Combine in a small saucepan, mustard seeds, sugar, celery seeds, vinegar, cinnamon, cloves, cumin seeds, peppercorns, cayenne, dry mustard and salt.

4. Allow to boil. Stir until sugar dissolves. Remove from heat and set aside. Strain the spice-infused vinegar into the tomatoes.

5. Cook for a further 20 minutes, constantly stirring. Season with salt to your preference. Allow to cool. Store in clean jars.

Jalapeno Ketchup

Delicious tomato ketchup with a classic taste and an addition of Jalapeno for an extra kick.

Yield: 3 cups

Time: 25 minutes

Ingredients:

- Cider vinegar (1/4 cup)
- Dark brown sugar (1/3 cup)
- Tomato paste (16 oz.)
- Tomato sauce (18 oz.)
- Jalapeno pepper (1)
- Vegetable oil (2 tsp.)

Directions:

1. Jalapenos must be seeded and finely diced. Meanwhile, pour vegetable oil in a small saucepan over medium high heat. Add jalapeno.

2. Cook for about 2 minutes. Add in tomato paste, tomato sauce, cider vinegar, and brown sugar. Bring to a boil.

3. Cook for about 10 minutes or until mixture is reduced to ½. Remove saucepan from heat and let it cool.

Ginger and Coriander Ketchup

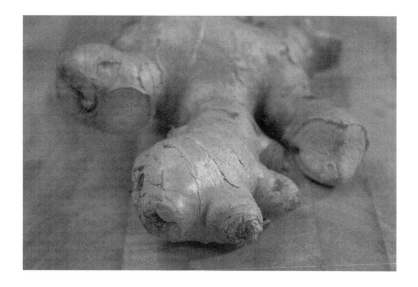

When dolloped on steak, this ketchup will blow your mind.

Yields: 1 pint

Time: 1 hour 45 minutes

Ingredients:

- Brown sugar (1/3 cup)
- Red wine vinegar (3/4 cup + 2 tbsp.)
- Tomatoes (2 lbs., yellow or orange)
- Ground black pepper and salt (1 tsp.)
- Cloves (2)
- Coriander seeds (1 tbsp.)
- Fresh basil leaves
- Fresh red chili
- Garlic (2 cloves)
- Thumb-sized fresh ginger
- Olive oil
- Celery (1 stick)
- Bulb fennel (1/2)
- Red onion (1 large)

Directions:

1. Chop roughly, the red onion, celery, bulb fennel, and fresh ginger. Chop the yellow or orange tomatoes as well.

2. Combine in a large saucepan, all the vegetables. Add olive oil, garlic, chili, ginger, cloves, basil stalks and coriander seeds.

3. Sprinkle with salt and pepper. Cook for about 15 minutes. Pour the tomatoes and water.

4. Bring to a boil until mixture is reduced by half. Add in basil leaves. Pour into a food processor, then transfer into a clean pan.

5. Drizzle with sugar and vinegar. Once desired consistency is achieved, pour into sterilized bottles.

Fresh Whey Ketchup

Have you ever thought of making fermented ketchup, well, here is a perfect recipe for you?

Yield: 1 pint

Time: 5 minutes (3-5 days for fermentation)

Ingredients:

- Ground cloves (1/2 tsp.)
- Allspice (1 tsp.)
- Salt (1 tsp.)
- Raw apple cider vinegar (2 tbsp.)
- Fresh whey (1/4 cup + 2 tbsp.)
- Honey (1/4 cup)
- Tomato paste (2 cup)

Directions:

1. Pour tomato paste into a mixing bowl. Then, fold in honey.

2. Add one-quarter cup fresh whey and sweetened tomato paste together with salt, cloves, allspice, and vinegar. Whisk continuously until mixture is smooth.

3. Pour ketchup into a glass container. Top with fresh whey and cover loosely. Store at room temperature for 3 to 5 days.

Kalamata Olive Ketchup

This makes a perfect finish for Mediterranean burgers or broiled fish.

Yield: 1 cup

Time: 5 minutes

Ingredients:

- Garlic (1/4 tsp.)
- Onion powder (1/2 tsp.)
- Parsley flakes (1/2 tsp.)
- Kalamata olives (2 tbsp., pitted)
- Ketchup (1/2 cup)

Directions:

1. Chop Kalamata olives and garlic into fine pieces.

2. Combine all the ingredients in a mixing bowl. Mix thoroughly. It can be served immediately.

3. Or, it can be placed inside sterilized containers and store up to 3 weeks.

Yellow Onion Ketchup

Sweet, spicy and tangy. This ketchup will entice you to skip the one bought from the store.

Yield: 1 pint

Time: 55 minutes

Ingredients:

- Molasses (1 tbsp.)
- Dark brown sugar (1/2 cup)
- Ground ginger (1/4 tsp.)
- Ground cayenne pepper (1/4 tsp.)
- Ground allspice (1/4 tsp.)
- Ground black pepper (1 1/2 tsp.)
- Salt (2 tbsp.)
- Cider vinegar (1/2 cup)
- Tomatoes (4 lb.)
- Yellow onion (1/2)
- Garlic (3 cloves)
- Olive oil (1 tbsp.)

Directions:

1. Dribble a medium saucepan with olive oil and cook onion for about 3 minutes. Add garlic and cook for another minute stirring consistently.

2. Pour vinegar, ginger, fish sauce, allspice, cayenne, salt, tomatoes, and black pepper. Cook for roughly 20 minutes.

3. Pour mixture into a blender and pulse until mixture is smooth. Strain well to remove seeds and skin.

4. Add molasses and brown sugar. Pour into saucepan and cook again for a further 25 minutes. Let it cool and transfer into clean jars.

Fresh Basil Ketchup

A delicious blend of fresh basil and tomato. Perfect with ravioli or spaghetti.

Yield: 500 ml

Time: 40 minutes

Ingredients:

- Brown sugar (70 g)
- Red wine vinegar (200 ml)
- Plum tomatoes (500 g)
- Ground black pepper (1 tsp.)
- Cloves (2)
- Coriander seeds (1 tbsp.)
- Fresh basil leaves (1 bunch)
- Red chili (1/2, fresh)
- Garlic (2 cloves)
- Ginger (1 thumb-size)
- Olive oil
- Celery (1 stick)
- Bulb fennel (1/2)
- Onion (1 large)

Directions:

1. In a large saucepan add olive oil and all vegetables, combine. Then add, garlic, basil, chili, coriander seeds, ginger, and cloves.

2. Sprinkle with salt and pepper. Cook over low heat for about 15 minutes. Add water and the tomatoes.

3. Boil until mixture is reduced to 1/2. Transfer into a food processor or blender. Pulse until mixture is smooth.

4. Dribble with sugar and vinegar. Again, pour into saucepan and simmer until mixture thickens. Spoon ketchup into prepared jars. Store in the fridge.

Sucanat Ketchup

The joy of making a delicious home-made ketchup with all the benefits of a lacto-fermented ingredient.

Yield: 1 cup

Time: 20 minutes

Ingredients:

- Sucanat (1/8 cup)
- Salt (1/4 tsp.)
- Pinch of cayenne pepper
- Pinch of allspice
- Pinch of cinnamon
- Dry mustard (1/4 tsp.)
- Garlic powder (1/4 tsp.)
- Onion powder (1/4 tsp.)
- Vinegar (2 tbsp.)
- Water (1/3 cup)
- Tomato paste (7 oz.)

Directions:

1. Blend sucanat into a blender and process to make it less crunchy.

2. Combine all the ingredients in a large mixing bowl. Mix well until smooth. Adjust seasonings.

3. Transfer ketchup into a sterilized jar and refrigerate.

Red Wine Vinegar Ketchup

An amazing homemade ketchup with a pleasant tangy flavour.

Yields: 4 cups

Time: 45 minutes

Ingredients:

- Bay leaves (3)
- Ground allspice (1/2 tsp.)
- Ground nutmeg (2 tbsp.)
- Olive oil (1/2 cup)
- Sugar (1/2 cup)
- Red wine vinegar (1 cup)
- Onion (1 large)
- Tomato paste (5.5 oz.)
- Tomatoes (28 oz., chopped)
- Salt and pepper to taste

Directions:

1. Chop the onion into tiny pieces. Then, put all the ingredients in a saucepan over medium heat.

2. Simmer for about 3 minutes. Cook and stir occasionally until the mixture has reduced to half, roughly 30 minutes.

3. Allow the ketchup to cool at room temperature. After which, pour it into a blender or food processor.

4. Once desired consistency is achieved, it can be served immediately.

Olive Oil and Cider Vinegar Ketchup

Homemade ketchup gives you the option to spice it up however you like. Here is one with added nutritional values.

Yields: 2 cups

Time: 3 hour 20 minutes

Ingredients:

- Salt (1/2 tsp.)
- Cider vinegar (1/2 cup)
- Dark brown sugar (2/3 cup)
- Tomato paste (1 tbsp.)
- Olive oil (2 tbsp.)
- Onion (1 medium)
- Whole tomatoes in puree (1 (28 oz.) Can)

Directions:

1. Pour the puree tomatoes in a blender. Blend until smooth. Meanwhile, cook onion in a saucepan over medium heat for about 8 minutes or until softened.

2. Add tomato paste, pureed tomatoes, vinegar, brown sugar, and salt. Leave uncovered and let it simmer.

3. Cook for about 1 hour or until mixture thickens. Remove from heat and let it cool. After which, pour into a blender and blend until smooth.

4. Transfer into a container and seal tightly. Chill for about 2 hours.

Worcestershire Sauce Ketchup

A gluten free recipe which tastes much better than what you get in the store.

Yields: 1 cup

Time: 15 minutes

Ingredients:

- Salt (1/8 tsp.)
- Cayenne pepper (1/4 tsp.)
- Garlic powder (1/2 tsp.)
- Dijon mustard (1 tsp.)
- Worcestershire sauce (1 tsp.)
- Brown sugar (1 tbsp.)
- Red wine vinegar (1/3 cup)
- Molasses (1/4 cup)
- Tomato paste (156 ml. Can)

Directions:

1. Combine all the ingredients in a saucepan. Allow to boil over medium low heat. Stir and simmer for about 4 minutes.

2. Remove from heat and set aside to cool.

3. Transfer into a sterilized jar and store in the fridge.

Sweet Spicy Ketchup

A ketchup with a 'zing.' Once you have made this sweet chili sauce, you will always be asking for more.

Yields: 2 liters

Time: 1 hour 20 minutes

Ingredients:

- Golden caster sugar (200g)
- White wine vinegar (200ml)
- Tabasco sauce (1/2 tsp.)
- Tomato puree (3 tbsp.)
- Tomatoes (2 kg., ripe)
- Celery salt (2 tsp.)
- Ground black pepper (1/2 tsp.)
- Allspice (1 tsp.)
- Cinnamon stick (1 short)
- Ground coriander (1 tsp.)
- Garlic (4 cloves)
- Olive oil (5 tbsp.)
- Celery (250g)
- Onions (4)

Directions:

1. Using a processor, chop celery, onions and ripe tomatoes. Meanwhile, dribble saucepan with olive oil.

2. Add onions and celery, cook for about 5 minutes. Add garlic, cook for an additional 5 minutes. Dribble with spices and cook for about 1 minute.

3. Add all the remaining ingredients.

4. Bring to a boil then simmer for about 1 hour. Whizz the mixture using a stick blender.

5. When mixture is smooth, put it back on heat and cook for another few minutes or until mixture is reduced.

6. Let it cool and put into a container or jar. Refrigerate.

Cayenne Pepper Ketchup

This ketchup is perfect for you if you are tired of eating boring, bland food.

Yields: 2 cups

Time: 1 hour 45 minutes

Ingredients:

- Brown sugar (1/4 cup)
- Red wine vinegar (3/4 cup)
- Fresh tomatoes (2 ½ lb.)
- Water (1 ½ cups)
- Fresh basil (1/4 cup)
- Cayenne pepper (1 tsp.)
- Pepper (1 pinch)
- Salt (1 pinch)
- Ground clove (2 tsp.)
- Garlic (2 cloves)
- Fresh ginger (2 tsp.)
- Red onion (2 ½)
- Olive oil (2 tbsp.)

Directions:

1. Dribble a large stock pot with olive oil over medium low heat and add all ingredients through cayenne pepper. Stir occasionally.

2. Add in water and simmer. Cook until mixture is reduced to half. Remove from heat and dribble with basil.

3. Pour into an immersion blender. Pulse until mixture is smooth. Transfer to a clean pan and add brown sugar and red wine.

4. Simmer until sauce is thicker. Adjust seasonings. Let it cool and pour into clean jars. Refrigerate.

Star Anise and Peppercorn Ketchup

This delicious ketchup is mildly spicy and slightly sweet.

Yield: 2 cups

Time: 35 minutes

Ingredients:

- 1 tablespoon Dijon mustard
- 1 tablespoon black mustard seeds
- 1 teaspoon ground paprika
- 1 teaspoon Szechuan peppercorns
- 2 star anise
- 2 tablespoons malt vinegar
- 3 tablespoons caster sugar
- 800g tomatoes
- fresh red chili
- groundnut oil
- 2 red onions

Directions:

1. Slice onions into thin pieces. Meanwhile, drizzle a heavy pan with some oil and add onions.

2. Cook for 5 minutes. Chop red chili and 600 grams of the tomatoes. After which, blitz the remainder in a blender or food processor.

3. Drizzle the onion with sugar and continue cooking until onions turn dark. Pour vinegar and add in chopped and blitzed tomatoes. Boil and add star anise.

4. Simmer for few minutes and add ground peppercorns and ground paprika. Pour in Dijon mustard and mustard seeds.

5. Sprinkle with salt and simmer for 15 minutes. Remove from heat and spoon into sterilized jars.

Teriyaki Ketchup

This is a great sauce, marinade or glaze. Many persons go crazy over its great taste.

Yields: 1 cup

Time: 5 minutes

Ingredients:

- Onion (1, green)
- White pepper (1/4 tsp.)
- Ginger (2 tsp., freshly grated)
- Garlic (1 clove)
- Teriyaki sauce (1/4 cup)
- Ketchup (1/2 cup)

Directions:

1. Mix all the ingredients in a medium bowl. Stir thoroughly to create a smooth mixture.

2. Pour into a sterilized jar and chill.

Chipotle Ketchup

This very simple, easy to make ketchup will outdo the store-bought condiments and is a great topping.

Yields: 1 cup

Time: 30 minutes

Ingredients:

- Garlic powder (1/8 tsp.)
- Onion powder (1/4 tsp.)
- Salt (3/4 tsp.)
- Chipotle paste (1 tsp.)
- Water (1/4 cup)
- White vinegar (1/2 cup)
- Honey (1/4 cup)
- Tomato paste (6 oz.)

Directions:

1. Combine all the ingredients in a saucepan over medium high heat. Mix until smooth. Simmer for about 20 minutes, stirring occasionally.

2. Remove pan from heat and set aside to cool. Store in the fridge inside a sterilized jar.

Chia Seed Ketchup

Combined with canned tomatoes and vinegar, the addition of the chia seeds it creates a luxurious, thick blend.

Yields: 2 cups

Time: 10 minutes

Ingredients:

- Chia seeds (1 tsp.)
- Pinch of cloves, cayenne pepper, allspice, cinnamon
- Mustard powder (1 tsp., dried)
- Salt (1 tsp.)
- Molasses (2 tbsp.)
- Honey (2 tbsp.)
- Onion powder (1 tbsp.)
- Garlic powder (1 tsp.)
- White vinegar (1/2 cup)
- Tomato paste (3 cans)

Directions:

1. Combine all the ingredients in a blender or food processor. Blend until mixture is smooth and reaches the desired consistency. Store in sterilized jars.

2. Place jars inside the fridge overnight or at least 2 hours.

Cinnamon and Bay Leaf Ketchup

A delicious combination of fresh tomatoes, ground spices and chile. An interesting taste that you cannot resist.

Yields: 3 cups

Time: 1 hour 15 minutes

Ingredients:

- Allspice (1/4 tsp.)
- Cloves (4 whole)
- Red pepper flakes (1/4 tsp.)
- Celery seeds (1/4 tsp.)
- Cinnamon (1 stick)
- Bay leaf (1)
- Salt (1 ½ tsp.)
- Brown sugar (5 tbsp.)
- White vinegar (1/2 cup)
- Green chili (1 tbs.)
- Yellow onion (1 medium)
- Tomatoes (2 lb.)

Directions:

1. Roughly chop tomatoes, yellow onion and green chili.

2. Wrap cinnamon, allspice, cloves, bay leaf, celery seeds, and red pepper flakes in a triple layer medical gauze or double-layer cheesecloth. Tie it into a bundle. Set aside.

3. Combine onions, vinegar, brown sugar, salt, garlic, chili and tomatoes in a saucepan.

4. After which add the spice bundle. Cook for about 45 minutes.

5. Remove spice bundle. Puree the mixture in a blender until smooth and strain.

6. Transfer to a pot and cook over medium low heat until it thickens. Store in the fridge.

Molasses and Agave Nectar Ketchup

Molasses and Agave, a great choice for a healthy ketchup.

Yield: 2 cups

Time: 2 hours 10 minutes

Ingredients:

- 2 1/2 cups water
- 1 teaspoon agave nectar
- 1 teaspoon molasses
- 1 teaspoon salt
- 1/4 teaspoon allspice
- 1 tablespoon onion powder
- 1 tablespoon garlic powder
- 4 tablespoons brown sugar
- 1/2 cup white vinegar
- 2 6-ounce cans tomato paste

Directions:

1. Combine all the ingredients in a pot over medium low heat. Let it simmer and cook for about 2 hours.

2. Once desired consistency is achieved, remove from heat and let it cool. Transfer into ketchup bottles or jars.

Sauerkraut Juice Ketchup

Sauerkraut juice ketchup, a great lacto-fermented option. Its subtle, tangy taste will entice your taste bud.

Yield: 3 cups

Time: 10 minutes

Ingredients:

- A pinch of cayenne pepper
- 2 1/4 teaspoons salt
- 6 tablespoons sauerkraut juice
- 3 small garlic cloves
- 3 tablespoons raw apple cider vinegar
- 1/3 cup honey
- 3 7-ounce cans tomato paste

Directions:

1. In a mixing bowl, combine all the ingredients. Mix well to combine all the ingredients thoroughly.

2. Pour into sterilized jars. Wipe the top portion of the jar. Seal tightly and leave at room temperature.

3. Allow 3 days for it to ferment. After which, store in the fridge.

Dates Ketchup

This smooth tomato condiment is the perfect dipping sauce for your favorite finger foods.

Yields: 1 cup

Time: 4 hours

Ingredients:

- tomato paste (6 oz.)
- water (1/4 cup)
- apple cider vinegar (2 tbsp.)
- ginger (1/4 tsp.)
- cloves (2 pinches)
- cinnamon (1/4 tsp.)
- allspice (1/4 tsp.)
- salt (1/2 tsp.)
- garlic (2 cloves)
- green smith apples (2)
- onion (1 small)

Directions:

1. Place all ingredients in a slow cooker. Cook the mixture for about 4 hours.

2. Let the mixture cool then place it in a blender. Blend until desired consistency is achieved. Store inside glass containers.

Green Smith Apple Ketchup

This smooth tomato condiment is the perfect dipping sauce for your favorite finger foods.

Yields: 1 cup

Time: 4 hours

Ingredients:

- tomato paste (6 oz.)
- water (1/4 cup)
- apple cider vinegar (2 tbsp.)
- ginger (1/4 tsp.)
- cloves (2 pinches)
- cinnamon (1/4 tsp.)
- allspice (1/4 tsp.)
- salt (1/2 tsp.)
- garlic (2 cloves)
- green smith apples (2)
- onion (1 small)

Directions:

1. Place all ingredients in a slow cooker. Cook the mixture for about 4 hours.

2. Let the mixture cool then place it in a blender. Blend until desired consistency is achieved. Store inside glass containers.

Banana Ketchup

This is a popular Philippine fruit ketchup condiment. Perfect for your omelets, hot dogs, fish, grilled pork or even your fries.

Yield: 1 ½ cups

Time: 45 minutes

Ingredients:

- bay leaf (1)
- soy sauce (1 tsp.)
- teaspoon salt (1/8 tsp.)
- ground clove (1/8 tsp.)
- black pepper (1/2 tsp.)
- dark brown sugar (2 tbsp.)
- water (1/4 cup)
- apple cider vinegar (1/2 cup)
- ripe bananas (2 large)
- tomato paste (1 tbsp.)
- Serrano chilis (4)
- garlic (2 cloves)
- yellow onion (1 small)
- annatto seeds (3/4 tsp.)
- canola oil (2 tbsp.)

Directions:

1. Combine annatto seeds and oil over medium heat in a medium saucepan. Let it cool for 1 minute and discard seeds.

2. Cook onion over medium heat for about 5 minutes. Add garlic and chile, cook for an additional minute. Pour tomato paste, then cook until mixture turns orange red.

3. Add banana and mix well. Pour water, vinegar, pepper, sugar, salt, clove, bay leaf, and soy sauce. Allow to boil and cook for roughly 30 minutes. Let it cook and discard bay leaf. Pour mixture into a food processor. Adjust seasonings. Store in a jar and refrigerate.

Fresh Blueberry Ketchup

Exceptionally easy and perfect for a Summer barbecue.

Yield: 3 cups

Time: 5 hours

Ingredients:

- ground pepper (1/4 tsp.)
- salt (1/4 tsp.)
- lime juice (1 tbsp.)
- fresh ginger (2 tbsp.)
- red wine vinegar (1/2 cup)
- sugar (1 ¼ cups)
- shallot (1 medium)
- fresh blueberries (2 ½ cups)

Directions:

1. In a saucepan, combine lime juice, ginger, vinegar, sugar, blueberries, salt and pepper, set over medium heat.

2. Add in sugar and let dissolve. Simmer for about 25 minutes or until mixture thickens.

3. Transfer into sterilized jars and refrigerate for about 4 hours.

Yellow Curry Ketchup

A traditional German recipe, with a delicate, spicy and aromatic curry flavour.

Yield: 1 cup

Time: 1 hour 5 minutes

Ingredients:

- apple cider vinegar (1/4 cup)
- brown sugar (1/2 cup)
- tomatoes (1 (28 oz.) can, with juice)
- red pepper flakes (1/2 tsp.)
- ground allspice (1/4 tsp.)
- a pinch of ground cloves
- smoked paprika (1/2 tsp.)
- ground mustard (1 tsp.)
- ground yellow curry (1 tbsp.)
- salt (1 tsp.)
- tomato paste (1 tbsp.)
- garlic (4 cloves)
- olive oil (2 tbsp.)

Directions:

1. Dribble a medium pan with oil and set over medium heat. Following, sauté onions for about 5 minutes, add the garlic and cook for 1 minute. Pour in tomato paste. Dribble with all the spices and salt. Stir well.

2. Add crush tomatoes, sugar and vinegar. Combine well and simmer for about 45 minutes until mixture thickens, continue stirring. Transfer from heat to an immersion blender and blend.

3. After blending, strain the mixture into a clean pan. Adjust seasonings and store in sterilized jars.

Garlic Ketchup

This garlic ketchup condiment will make your French fries extra yummy.

Yield: 2 cups

Time: 30 minutes

Ingredients:

- fresh oregano leaves (2 tsp.)
- garlic (3 cloves)
- tomato paste (6 oz.)
- apple cider vinegar (1 tbsp.)
- water (1/2 cup)
- dates (6)

Directions:

1. Combine the dates and water together. Pour in the mixture to a saucepan and add the remaining ingredients. Heat the mixture, whisking occasionally

2. Remove pan from heat and put aside to cool. Transfer into sterilized jars and store in the fridge.

Peach Ketchup

Peach Ketchup, sweet and tangy. A perfect marinade for pork and chicken and a great dip for your sweet potato fries.

Yield: 1 cup

Time: 30 minutes

Ingredients:

- white wine vinegar (60 ml)
- brown sugar (1 tbsp.)
- cinnamon (1/4 tsp.)
- curry powder (1/2 tsp.)
- tomato paste (1 tbsp.)
- bay leaves (2)
- sunflower oil (1 tbsp.)
- peaches (500g)
- red chili pepper (1/2 large)
- garlic (2 cloves)
- shallot (1)

Directions:

1. Peel both the shallot and garlic clove, add chili pepper and chop them finely. Halve peaches and chop coarsely. Then, dribble some oil in a medium pot. Sauté shallot, garlic, shallot, and chili pepper.

2. Add the curry powder, brown sugar, bay leaves, tomato paste and cinnamon, and roast shortly until the mixture gets darker. Drizzle vinegar and add chopped peaches. Cook over medium-low heat for about 15 minutes. Stir constantly.

3. Discard bay leaves and pour puree into a blender. Blend until desired consistency is achieved. Adjust seasonings.

Nutmeg Ketchup

Use this tasty nutmeg ketchup to spice up your next egg dish or bean burger.

Yield: 2 cups

Time: 55 minutes

Ingredients:

- bay leaves (2)
- ground allspice (2 pinches)
- nutmeg (2 heaped tsp.)
- olive oil (1/2 cup)
- sugar (1/2 cup)
- red wine vinegar (1 cup)
- onion (1 large)
- tomato paste (1 can)
- tomatoes (1 can)

Directions:

1. Chop the onions and tomatoes. Combine in a saucepan. Simmer over medium high heat and cook for 45 minutes until the mixture is reduced to 1/2.

2. Use an immersion blender to puree mixture. Let it cool before transferring to a sterilized jar.

Cranberry Ketchup

Use this tasty nutmeg ketchup to spice up your next egg dish or bean burger.

Yield: 2 cups

Time: 55 minutes

Ingredients:

- bay leaves (2)
- ground allspice (2 pinches)
- nutmeg (2 heaped tsp.)
- olive oil (1/2 cup)
- sugar (1/2 cup)
- red wine vinegar (1 cup)
- onion (1 large)
- tomato paste (1 can)
- tomatoes (1 can)

Directions:

1. Chop the onions and tomatoes. Combine in a saucepan. Simmer over medium high heat and cook for 45 minutes until the mixture is reduced to 1/2.

2. Use an immersion blender to puree mixture. Let it cool before transferring to a sterilized jar.

Conclusion

Wow we did it! Thank you for sticking through all the way the end of this Easy Recipes Cookbook with us. We hope you enjoyed all 30 delicious and easy ketchup recipes that are easy to make and simply delicious.

So, what happens next?

Nothing breathes perfection like practice. So, keep on cooking and enjoying new and exciting meals with your whole family. Then whenever you are ready for another spark of delicious inspiration grab another one of our books and let us continue our culinary journey together.

Remember, drop us a review if you loved what you read and until we meet again, keep on cooking delicious food.

Author's Afterthoughts

Thanks Ever So Much to Each of My Cherished Readers for Investing the Time to Read This Book!

I know you could have picked from many other books but you chose this one. So, big thanks for buying this book and reading all the way to the end.

If you enjoyed this book or received value from it, I'd like to ask you for a favor. Please take a few minutes to post an honest and heartfelt review on **Amazon.** Your support does make a difference and helps to benefit other people.

Thank you!

Carla Hale

About the Author

Carla Hale

I think of myself as a foodie. I like to eat, yes. I like to cook even more. I like to prepare meals for my family and friends, I feel like that's what I was born to do...

My name is Carla Hale and as may have suspected already, I am originally from Scotland. I am first and foremost a mother, a wife, but simultaneously over the years I became a proclaimed cook. I have shared my recipes with many and will continue to do so, as long as I can. I like different. I dress different, I love different, I speak different and I cook different. I like to think that I am different because I am more animated about what I do than most; I feel more and care more.

It served me right when cooking to sprinkle some tenderness, love, passion, in every dish I prepare. It does not matter if I am preparing a meal for strangers passing by my cooking booth at the flea market or if I am making my mother's favorite recipe. Each and every meal I prepare from scratch will contain a little bite of my life story and little part of my heart in it. People feel it, taste it and ask for more! Thank you for taking the time to get to know me and hopefully through my recipes you can learn a lot more about my influences and preferences. Who knows you might just find your own favorite within my repertoire! Enjoy!

Printed in Great Britain
by Amazon

53445474R00050